before/after

By the same Author:

toxic/empathy (2024)

Amusements of Solitude – 180th Anniversary Edition; Alexander Herald (2024) Contributor: Foreword & Family History

before/after

J L Herald

before/after

Copyright © 2024 JL Herald

All rights reserved.

 A catalogue record for this work is available from the National Library of Australia

This book or any portion thereof may not be reproduced or used in any manner whatsoever without the express written permission of the copyright owner, except for the use of brief quotations in a book review.

First Printed 2024
by Yellow Gerbera Publishing
Australia

Cover Design © JL Herald 2024

Illustrations by Natassja Stamp (Tassji_S)

ISBN: 978-0-645991543 (paperback)

Website: http://www.JLHerald-poet.com

For Kayleigh

for all the children lost

all the parents left behind

Preface

As a person, a mother, who lost a child – I do not know if there is anything worse than the pain, the self-recrimination, the absolute empty deep abyss that becomes a part of you from the moment your child passes until you pass yourself. It is a grief that never seems to leave, its presence in your life is forever.

It is with this that I write these words. We are part of a group that no-one wants to be part of and we would want no one to join. The before – life that was with your precious child, and the after – how you go on, how you manage the yawning pit of emptiness that has appeared.

This is my story, but also the story of others that have been here before me, and those who are yet to come. Be gentle to yourself.

This book may be difficult to read for some, it delves into stages of grief, suicidal ideation, pain, loss and despair. But it also celebrates a life lived even as short as it was, and the memories that still exist.

The before where they existed

The before when they were happy

The before when you could not imagine

Your life without them in it

The after when they are gone

The after where there's a hollow

The after where nothing makes any sense

Your life going on when theirs is over

Contents

Before

Hello	15
Blue Eyes	16
Pancakes	17
Row Row	18
Cheeky	20
Moosie	22
Skywards	24
Face Plant	25
Sacrifice	27
Challenge	28
Rats	29
Chocolate Box	31
Midnight	32
Sleepwalker	33
Spaghetti Girl	34
Silly Songs	37
Dragons	39

Between

Breathe	41
Red Blue	43
Hope	44
Goodbye	46
Not the Same	48
Numb	49
Monday	50
Reality Bites	51
Confronting	52
Sunset	53
Fuck Off	56

Aromas	58
Grateful	60
No Words	61
Doves	63
Funeral	64

AFTER

Grief	69
Somebody	73
Return	77
Too Hard	79
Regret	82
The Tree	83
Silence	86
Guilt	88
Hot	90
Hole	91
Why Her?	92
Ghosts	94
Cracks	95
Memories	96
Star Dust	97
Cruelty	99
Echoes	101
Butterfly	104
Final Goodbye	105
She Was	106

Before

The time where life seems joyous and bright

The interlude between birth and forever

The stage where tomorrow is filled with promise

The era where love is without measure

Hello

you came into the world
and greeted it with a sneeze
the tiniest thing I've ever seen
my love for you immediate

cleaned up quickly, swaddled in pink
my little girl - she was perfect
we fell asleep, just her and me
snuggled together in the blankets

Blue Eyes

her eyes stare into mine

deep oceanic blue

absolute trust

burgeoning love

deep within azure depths

my eyes stare back in hers

a new life just started

already the spark of spirit

calm inquisitiveness

a butterfly's essence

a gentle calmness

a life of possibilities

drifting on future winds

wrapped in a tiny human

staring deep into my soul

Pancakes

old time tunes playing

salt and pepper shakers wiggling

strawberries jumping

mushrooms flipping

a single banana pivots

in a conga line of food

those delicious pancakes

ice cream oozing on the screen

olden time phone receivers

placed on a bearded mans ears

a ritzy lady smile lazily

holding a fork up high

her eyes glued

feet twitching

that advertisement had her raptured

pancake parlour for the win!

Row Row

her pony rears
        high into the air
teetering on the edge of calamity

her face split into a wide grin
        peal of laughter
air filled with bubbles of joy

her legs grip tight
        fat brown belly squeezed
reins gripped taut in hand

she masterfully controls
        fast plunging descent
holding on, not falling once

her pony kicks
        swinging wildly skywards
she leans into the saddle

absolutely sure of her control
        thrilled smile displaying delight
riding her rocking horse

Cheeky

an afternoon spent with grandpa

lolling on the grass watching

his granddaughters at play

supervising a day of fun

climbing slowly up the ladder

of the green painted slide

slip sliding down

running back to climb

waiting patiently for

her younger sister to ascend

side eyed look at grandpa

she starts to grin

a wide beaming smile

as she leaps off the end

her sliding forgotten

grandpa is more interesting

sidling over

face splitting

showing tiny baby teeth

bends over quickly

and bites grandpas toe!

Moosie

Piercing scream echoing over
plants and vegetable seedlings
the horrified stares of others
wondering if help is needed.

Anguished sobs soar higher
distress emanating soul deep
Moosie's little black eye
bitten off, creating shrieks.

Calming down her wailing
reminding Moosie has survived
many previous operations
sewn together many times.

His antlers held together
with black thread, hope and tears
while the stuffing in his leg
had been falling out for years.

Trying to find a replacement
proved an impossible mission
so Moosie lived out his days
a pen end for an eye missing.

Skywards

temptation beckons

as woolly clouds hang high

the tree standing, resplendent

wide branches enticing

offering excitement

drawing in, tempting

discovering hidden ladders

each rung tested

as they scale upwards

secret staircases revealed

as spring turns to autumn

winter chases summer

new challenges designed

as they attempt to find the way

to try and touch the sun

Face Plant

Schreeeech!

brakes gripping

slowing down metre by metre

brakes set poorly

distance to stop endless

Santa had been generous

new bike gleaming in the sun

to borrow, to have fun

to see what can be done

racing up high, top of the yard

zooming down, pedalling fast

slamming on those brakes

before the end wall was too late

flipping over on ones' arse

almost eating dirt

almost losing too much skin

that bike it stopped so fast

let's do it all again!

Sacrifice

that's not very motherly of you!

hand on heart, acting out the part

while standing on the rug

the movie playing on tv

strutting around

pretending she was the dragon

giving up it's life

for the ungrateful son

yet every time that Dragonheart was on

she knew what was coming

the dragon's final sacrifice

giving up its life

so that others may live

each time it played she cried

for the dragon only wanted love

and its desire to help

only ended with death

Challenge

I'm going to beat you this time! she yelled
as other cars flashed passed fast
throwing items at each other
trying to get out in front
get of my way! she screamed
driving recklessly without care
spinning off the road, skidding
holding in her great despair
zipping back onto the tarmac
dodging bullets tossed around
ramming into turtles
as she tried to chase him down
as last the finish line's in view
she almost grabbed the lead
but suddenly out of nowhere
a banana skin stops her speed
Lucas wins! he does it again
she throws her remote in disgust
new challenge made — a rainbow road
many afternoons playing Mario Kart

Rats

having fun scaring Kiki
about rats upon the ground
using them to make your sister
jump up when she fell down

frightening little Kiki
of the animals that scare
saying rats are on the floor
about to bite her hair!

those rats they got everywhere
outside and in the house
using it to get little Kiki
to be as quiet as a mouse.

rats on the bedroom floor
rats hiding in the cupboard
making sure Kiara stays in bed
sleeping with her head covered

the rats they weren't real
the rats were just a scare
but poor little baby sister
thought she was their dinner

Chocolate Box

the school they gave us both

a box of chocolates full

filled to the brim with mars

chocolate freddo frogs caramel

we'd thought these chocolates were given free

an award for good things done selflessly

so, we hid those special chocolates

deep beneath our beds

gooey melty chocolately goodness

sugar rush scrambling our heads

bars and packets litter the carpet

as we try to hide the mess

but the school they rang our mother

asking her for profits made

oops, we did not realise

those chocolates must be paid

Midnight

a warm muggy night

crickets chirps echo

dark expanse of night

filled with milky way

brightly shining before moonrise

in the quiet

a door shushes

soft tiptoed steps

across day warmed concrete

cool night breeze

of summer nights caressing skin

the vast expanse of the universe

filling eyes and mind

the creak of springs

arms stretched high

knees poised in flight

trampoling at midnight

Sleepwalker

creaking of an opening door

the snick as it closed softly

it's almost midnight; dark outside

I wonder who that could be

wandering out to look outside

up the driving walking

Kayleigh slowly padding road-wards

clearly half asleep, not talking

calling out her name, confused

where do you think you're going?

I have to give Alexandra her clothes

she needs them for a party

telling her to come back to bed

Alex can wait until sunrise

in the morning — has no memory

of her sleepwalking up the drive

Spaghetti Girl

thick squidgy noodles

bathed in gluggy thick red sauce

nestled tight snug inside

small aluminium cans

lined up in rows

four by two

waiting to be chosen

for a final journey

zipped up in a pocket

of polyester rayon

and ink-stained blotches

of connector pens forgotten

loose paper with scribbled doodles

and a teaspoon

sometimes many teaspoons

raided from the kitchen

no sandwiches of sugar jam

or vegemite lightly smeared

on heavily slathered butter

nor croissants of ham and cheese

pickles and salad leaves

just a single can of spaghetti

was all a girl could want

was all a girl would need

Silly Songs

singing silly songs at night

about twinkling little stars in flight

making up some silly lines

of Kiara buying rusty cars

these silly songs were made ad hoc

made up while singing on the spot

these silly songs just made us laugh

'bout driving cars on toes and arse

every night before sleep occurred

we all sang songs with silly words

as twinkling little twinkle stars

remind us who we are

Dragons

Icy talons raised,
> defiant and proud.

Fiery scales glowing,
> burning and fierce

Wide wings spread,
> skyward beckoning

The fire and the ice,
> dragons are forever

Between

The period between their passing and funeral

The part where everything's numb

The time where you're sure it's all a bad dream

The phase when you hope you're wrong

Breathe

breathe

oh please, breathe

one, one thousand, two, one thousand

breathe

just breathe

compress, compress one two three

breathe

come on sweetie

just one breath

just for mum

don't just lie there staring

breathe

come on, oh please come on

gasp, inhale

just one

make your chest rise

compress, compress, compress

breathe

god-damn it

breathe

breathe

please, please, please just breathe

please

breathe

Red Blue

       red

            blue

   blue

       red

strobing lights they never end

      blue

          red

red

   blue

help was here, they'd finally come

       red

         blue

   blue

       red

help my girl please ambulance men

Hope

Lying in that hospital bed
monitors, cables, and machines
all these impersonal instruments
keeping you here with me

I hold out hope and I hold your hand
I hope to any deity around
that you will soon be waking up
before long, your voice will sound

The hours and hours and hours pass
day turning into night
and still, I keep believing
that you are going to be alright

I cannot envisage anything
but you coming home soon with us
there is no way imaginable
you dying I will not discuss

I sit in quiet, the machines breathing
nurses and doctors by your side
Watching, hoping, praying, pleading
my hopes are not going to be denied.

Goodbye

The decision had been made
everything had been examined
your brain was starved of oxygen
large parts of it were damaged

We tried so hard to save you
but you were not going to survive
I made the choice to turn off
the machines keeping you alive

The doctors — they were quiet
turning off the things that beeped
giving instructions softly
as I lay my head against your cheek

I whispered that I loved you
as your chest — its motion ceased
and watched the monitors closely
the flat line that was your heartbeat

They called your death at 9:45
and I felt so very empty
my sunshine girl was gone forever
in her place there was just

nothing

Not the Same

Walking through the shopping centre
the day after she passed away

Looking at all those happy people
shopping, eating, drinking coffee

Don't they know that the world today
is not the world of yesterday

That the world that they woke to up
has fundamentally changed

I feel numb and I feel nothing
but a building sense of rage

How can all these people be smiling
when my world is not the same

Numb

I cannot feel, I do not feel, I am without feeling
I lie upon this couch staring at the ceiling

My mind a-mess, my mind a-roiling
processing anguish is far too torturing

So I become numb and I become blank
the great abyss inside has made my mind black

I cannot move, I do not think, I am without thought
tiny little whispers are leaving me distraught

I need blocks, I need walls, to keep this pain inside
I do not want these memories I do not want this pall

I just want to lay here unmoving
not feeling anything at all

Monday

those staring faces

hands held up, covering mouths

pointing fingers and shocked expressions

the feeling of nakedness

visual emotional bruising

exposed trauma out in the open

everyone knowing, everyone seeing

outwardly held together

by peeling sticky tape

hastily applied staples

and sheer will of mind

inside - roiling blackness

but unable to let it show

all those school kids and teachers

knowing of your pain

unable to express their disbelief

as you wander past their midst

spreading knowledge through rumours

whispered conversations

that she was forever gone

Reality Bites

the phone call I must make
I just don't want to do
I don't want this to be real
I don't want this to go through

reaching for the phone
putting it back down
not wanting to make the call
not wanting to move along

picking up the phone again
the numbers entered in
hesitating to press on send
the pain churning deep within

erasing the digits swiftly,
setting the phone aside,
pacing the room in turmoil,
dreading the final goodbye.

summoning the strength at last,
pushing through the dread,
dialling the funeral parlour,
to set the date ahead.

Confronting

nothing can ever prepare you
for the glossy magazine spread
of different types of coffins
coloured satins to lay her head

having to make choices
and having to decide
which one will she rest within
her final bed — it must be right

choosing white for her pure heart
and blue satin for her soul
knowing once the decision is made
is one more step closer towards the cold

Sunset

She stops in the open doorway
the vision in front — confronting
the open coffin upon the dais
background music softly playing

She knows she rests up there within
the light that was snuffed out
but still, she cannot move towards
she cannot handle the sight

She pulls herself together
takes a deep breath and walks on
to look upon her sleeping face
these last moments with her sun

Her white t-shirt, her favourite skirt
odd socks and bubble-gum shoes
and nestled within her shortened hair
a silver butterfly threaded through

She gazes at the sun that's set
reaches in to hold her hand
the unmoving, stiff, and cold fingers
grasping reflex now vanished

Her heart is breaking, her soul destroyed
her thoughts utterly overwhelmed
that this will be the final time
her sun was going to be beheld

She leaned into the void that was
kissed her smooth and cold forehead
whispering she was so very sorry
her cheek pressed against her head

The time has passed, it was time to leave
one last time she looked upon
her sunshine girl — so cold alone
her radiance now darkened

Alone again in her eternal bed
coffin cover screwed down tight
and never again would the sun within
bring its lightness to the night.

Fuck Off

why does this woman think
she has any right to say
my daughter's in a better place
instead of being here with me today

how dare she try to stop me
how dare she bring her righteous squad
how dare she tell me all about
my daughter being with her god

I'm not religious, I have never believed
I do not attend your church
I do not know why you're doing this
but your presence is a scourge

my anger and my rage increase
as you drone on about your praying
you cannot see it — my appalled expression
your lack of empathy is dismaying

on and on and on you chatter
how I reconnect with my daughter
if I want to see or hear her again
I must become your Gods supporter

get out of my face and go away
fuck off with your proselytizing
using my grief to manipulate me
is truly and utterly despising

Aromas

I have the entire flower shop

I swear there's nothing left

every conceivable type of flower

every florist shop bereft

roses, gerberas, babies breath

orchids, lilies, tulips too

every single imaginable colour

yet sorrow lingers through

the cloying scent of floral wreaths

the overwhelming stench

of piles and piles and piles of flowers

decaying and dying on my bench

Grateful

tragedy has a funny way

of showing who cares

from people you've never met

or friends long past not heard

even in the blackness

sympathy and love is felt

and although I may not have said

we were grateful to the crowd

the food, the flowers,

      the thoughts and prayers

the kindness that was shown

our tragedy brought love together

and love was felt and known

No Words

Staring at the blank paper
Trying to find the words
How could I ever encapsulate
Her life, her love, her person

I sit and stare, the blankness mocks
The words - they just won't come
A mental block, my grief too great
To ever prepare the tome

Days on days to formulate
Unending empty sheets
No words were flowing from my pen
Her eulogy incomplete

Her final day it came so quick
Words stuck inside my head
I just can't do it — not at all
I cannot find the verse

At last it came, my time to speak
My time to tell the world of her
I had no words upon the sheet
Only empty white incomplete

I looked down at my blank paper
Surely her life was something
Closed my eyes and took a breath
and glanced at her white coffin

I stood upfront; the words poured out
Spoken straight from heart to mouth
Every detail, expressed eloquently
Recounting her life, her love, her person

I spoke at length of my love for her
From her first breath to her last
My love was going to continue
Until my final breath was passed.

Doves

soft feathers

white under fingers

quiet coos thrum

black eyes peer skywards

releasing — the dove flies

soaring cloud-wards

wind lifting

her   soul

forever

free

Funeral

Starkly white coffin,
floral display of white and blue.
All the seats are taken,
standing — there's no room.
A massive crowd of people
come to say farewell.
People sitting in the aisles,
outside there's still a queue.

All these people were silent
as her eulogy let fly.
Her life displayed in photographs
as we thought on why things die.
Her mother and her siblings spoke,
Mr Haidons' words multiply.
Then the moment came
to say our last goodbye.

Her coffin gently lowered

sound of her favourite song

Tears — they started falling,

as our hearts they did go on.

People hugged each other

as reminiscences commenced.

Slowly filing past where

at last she was at rest.

There was just one last thing to say

as the funeral finally ended

a sprinkle of personality

Kayleigh's little touch

the very last word was had

as we filed out the doors

thanks so much 'god' for doing this

fuck you so very much.

The three songs we played at the funeral were:

Let It Die · Foo Fighters
Echoes, Silence, Patience & Grace
© 2008 Roswell/RCA

My Heart Will Go On · Celine Dion
Titanic Soundtrack
© 1997 Columbia Records and Epic Records

Fuck You · Lily Allen
It's Not Me, It's You
© 2009 Parlophone Records Ltd

After

The cycle of grieving has started

The chapter of life after their demise

The point you realise they're not coming home

That you've said your very last goodbye

Grief

concealed sphere of torment within
delicate crystal, bubble reminiscent
precariously held, unstable existence
fractured cracks test surface resistance
confined by fragility - a smoky haze resides
a nebulous cacophony of memories inside
amorphous, churning, agitation fluctuating
hurt, pain, love, fear, sorrow unending

small fissures permit smoky tendrils escape
ruminations, images, form and reshape
extending hazy fingers clutching
encircling aortic membranes crushing
darkness beckons inviting remembrance
memories made, memories lost, anguish
healing thoughts, cracked glass melding
hindering, preventing shadows overwhelming

unexpected shock shatters

splintered fragments scattered

shredding protective barriers

exposing mind and heart to darkness

roiling blackened smoke enshrouded

obscuring sunlight smothering soul

distressed reminiscences strangling joy

the abyss calls

temptation to fall

enticed by pain's termination

tormented memories suffocating persuasion

eaten by guilt, ravaged by grief

swirling, choking, overpowering misery

reaching through the darkness churning

a gentle breeze of love and of caring

encircling arms providing needed refuge

safety from the pull of desolation's deluge

anchored by today not thoughts of past pain

healing reflections rebuilding reclaimed

layers of crystal expanding, re-forming

strengthening, reinforcing

the shield from ones' torment

Somebody

it seems like only yesterday
that you were here with us
telling off your brothers
and creating quite a fuss

you were so full of life and loving
caring about everything
it seems too cruel that you were taken
and left us here with this

we tried so hard to save you
to bring you back to us
although we tried absolutely everything
it was not to be enough

when the doctor said your heart was there
but your soul had gone away
I only thought about your life
if I could turn back time — just a day

but we are here and you are gone
never to return
we are left with sadness
and ask the question 'why her'

your friends were all heartbroken
you left them without warning
not a chance to say goodbye
not even just a reason

your teachers were left speechless
you were at school the day before
although they were there to teach you things
in fact you taught them more

but eventually their lives move on
and you become a memory
a schoolgirl friend they left behind
and eventually become a 'somebody'

somebody they once knew
somebody that passed away
somebody that they cared for
somebody – what's her name

they do not mean to forget you
life gets in the way
they have to keep on going on
they may remember you some day

for me your picture sits in a frame
I look at you each passing day
and though the colour slowly fades
my memory remains clear

I miss your smile, your bright blue eyes
your happiness and cheer
I also miss our arguments
as it meant you were still here

most of all I miss our talks
of me saying 'I love you'
and you looking back at me
saying 'Mum, I Love you too.'

Return

the words hung in the air
like a slow-moving calamity
of destruction pushing molecules
of oxygen out its way
as the impact of unempathy
burst into conscious reality
in the cacophony of misery
churning inside her head

those words spoken rapidly
of the horrible time he had
having to work extra hours
for extra pay for a time
how bad it was for him
as she had chosen to not be
at work so he was glad
she'd decided to return

those words shot through the air
halting thoughts inside her head

attempting to understand
the missing morality they contained
grappled with the meaning
tired mind silently screaming
as the clarity of his scheming
finally became crystal clear

he was angry that her tragedy
had resulted in disturbing
his well-ordered daily tasks
of inanity and insanity
lacking empathy and civility
decided to advise
one struggling with despondency
of his egotistical hide

the horror that arose
in her mind of tired woes
that this colleague was
a total fucking loss

so hastily responding

sarcastic words of apologies

I'll try to make sure this tragedy

never happens to you again

Too Hard

blindly staring indifferent
the manager up front talking
about timelines and deadlines
work that needs completing
concentration vanished into darkness
where hamsters titled loss and grief
are running wheels of insanity
images of stillness and lack of oxygen
death, coffins and decaying blossoms

a tear wells - gaining weight
its pearlescent reflection
hovers on the edge of oblivion
before rolling down into despair
a stifled sob stuck

other colleagues turn away
as anguish revealed
too hard to comprehend
avoidance is easy

words unspoken
eyes avoid meeting

team leaders discuss responsibilities
as she slips silently out the door
seeking refuge in an empty stairwell
sitting, curled tight
pressed against unfeeling concrete
in cold echoing silence
misery reflected in loneliness
separated by sorrow

Regret

Did I do the right thing

by turning off the machines?

Should I have held on longer?

Should I tried to be much stronger?

Were the doctors right

had her brain started to die?

Did I jump the gun?

Did I let her go too young?

Did I make the best choice

by choosing to turn them off?

In the end – I let her die

I just don't know if I was right.

The Tree

the tree I keep on looking at
the tree that speaks to me
the tree along the highway
that I pass at half past three

each day as I drive home from work
that tree is pictured in my mind
maybe today that tree and I
are going to be intertwined

as I pull onto the highway
press the accelerator to the floor
passing a hundred and twenty - thirty
as I keep pushing it for more

as I bear down on that tree ahead
visions flashing through my brain
my daughter cold and still and quiet
I'll never see her again

memories of her on the floor
eyes open, staring fixed
trying, hoping, praying, needing
I failed her – the thoughts persist

the pain that lies within my heart
sorrow overwhelms my soul
maybe that tree and I colliding
will stop the hurt and make me whole

but underneath the pain tsunami
my other children's faces rise
I cannot leave them – no, not today
my actions will destroy their lives

the tree it flashes past so quick
as another day I select to live
keep holding on just one more time
not let myself drown in grief

every day I drive along that road

that tree — it calls my name

and every day I must make the choice

that tree — or my life and pain

Silence

    The creak of unoiled door hinges

    the slam of a bag thrown onto tiles

    a rush of excitement ending with a hug

The door remains shut, never to open.

    The sound of footsteps on the garden path

    at three pm just after school

    excited murmurs of a day of fun

The path is quiet, no steps ever heard

    The clink of plates and cutlery

    place-mats laid; glasses filled

    counting knives, forks, spoons

Her place empty, the seat forever vacant

The churn of the washing machine
tumbled clothes folded neatly
sorted into piles for people to store

Her clothes unworn, draped in gathering dust

The touch of hand, shaking sleepy arms
parents awoken; there were things to be done
bright eyes, cheeky smile, restrained enthusiasm

Silence now fills the void where once she stood

Guilt

sometimes for a moment

I wonder while despondent

whether the world would be much better

if I was taken instead of her

if the person who's heart stopped beating

was her mother and not her being

would that have been an outcome

that was more acceptable to the world

the guilt is overwhelming

when watching a TV program

knowing she'll never be conscious

of how Harry Potter ends

how can I survive

to live a life of whys

doubting if my now existence

was worthy of her demise

the reaper took her away

I could not stand in his way

his scythe severing her life's string

but every day that I'm alive

I wonder and I cry

as guilt slowly eats my soul away

Hot

hot water beating down

standing, bent over

hot tears sliding

sound of the shower

muffled anguished sobs

stuck

choking

steam rises

tears mix with water

swirling eddies

drawing grief down

so I might face another day

Hole

how does one start to

come to terms that there will

always be a hole

where no hole should ever be?

where a space now exists

in your life and in your family

which should never have been?

how does one start to keep living

each day when that person-sized hole

once filled with a being

laughing, talking – just breathing

has ceased to exist

and you just have to accept

they are no longer there?

Why Her?

hatred – so much hatred
existing – over-existing
social accounts spewing vitriol
pitting man against bear against women
arguments over house cleaning
the role of a woman in a modern economy
discussions on body counts
      high value women
her body no longer within her decision

Blissful – fleeting happiness
excitement – simple enjoyment
a smile brought by a baby's laugh
a world once heartened by joyful delight
learning driven by a childs' enthusiasm
love unbound by fences of exclusion
why does hate survive?

was the butterfly of her existence
snuffed out unexpectedly

triggered by an anomaly
    of a time travelling oddity
why did her life end so suddenly
while hate and animosity
    endure and spread
like a virus of ongoing, relentless atrocities

why did the good and the pure die
why her and not those evils outside

Ghosts

her dressing gown still holds
the smell of her skin
the Pantene she had used
to wash her hair that past weekend
over a decade ago
yet her dressing gown still holds
the scent of her soul

burying my head
drawing her essence deep
into the recesses of my memories
the ghost of her smile
her arms hugging me close
her body snuggled to mine

tears flow
growing melancholy
her dressing gown packed away
maybe tomorrow
maybe next month
maybe in a year or so
her presence and the emptiness
can exist together
without wretching sadness

Cracks

porcelain
dried out after the monsoon
hardened into a mask

small tremors
shallow under earthen crust
shaking surface tension

a tiny uplift
creases and folds the surface
cracking the clay

a smile
lost for months, slowly rises
forgotten joy found

Memories

high on the back shelf
sits a box of forgotten
years settled in layers
of dust undisturbed
inside, a life lived, a life given
memories in the form of
cheap things and loose paper
a word, a scrap of material
a coloured in drawing of
a time fleeting, long past
the box sits, its presence
known but unacknowledged
as life moves onwards
as this life
once lived is tucked away
stored in darkness
its story ended
before it had begun

Star Dust

the universe exploded
a violent creation of star dust
swirling vortexes wildly spinning
unbound by concepts of time
in pure untamed energy

eons slipped, the earth - it turned
lifeforms rose and came and went
Many times built empires fell
as star dust drove it all

in every bird and snake and tree
in every house and nest and burrow
a speck of the first spark of life
is contained within it all

for every child that was born of us
for every parent that had been
passed along in every DNA strand
star dust underpins it all

eventually we all return to earth
and become what we once were
unlimited, unending star dust
for all eternity

Cruelty

sometime I really wonder
if people understand their words
are absolutely self-indulgent
as think they should have them heard
too many times others speak at me
as if their words are more important
that I should have gotten over
my grief for my lost daughter

these words they are not helpful
these words they are not right
these words are laced with cruelty
and malice and hateful spite
do others really think their opinion
holds more weight than mine
that I should feel so grateful
and take theirs as divine

my thoughts are not yours to own
your feelings are only yours

please do us both a favour
and keep your mouth secure
you telling someone that their grief
is causing you distress
how the hell do you think you're helping
by telling them to forget?

Echoes

her voice

unheard for over a decade

the timbre of her tones

the melody contained

words forgotten

yet held in a recording

left on an old phone

at the back of a drawer

her voice

once heard everyday

disappeared in history

now heard once more

echoes of yesterday

vibrating the air

causing tears to flow

love you Mummy

love you lots Mum

bye bye

Butterfly

deep within the rainforest
in dappled, shifting beams
an iridescent blue butterfly flits
amongst hibiscus and velvet leaves

fluttering between short moments
leaving small traces of its soul
with each flower that it touches
sharing love, kindness, and hope

the breeze gently lifts its wings
ascending above the canopy
the butterfly forever vanishes
existing now only in our memories

Final Goodbye

waves hissing softly across the sand

a light breeze rippling skirt hem

sun high above

a warm embrace

horizon

endless cloudless azure

waterfall of ash

like hourglass sand

tumbling white grey ochre

swirling

mingling with turquoise ocean

swept out

faint trail marking progress

ebbing waves pull seaward

as past memories arise

ashy streaks fade

slowly disappearing into the waves

the concluding act of the last farewell

her ashes scattered

given to the ocean

given to be free

She Was

She was …

    born of sunshine

bright joyful grin, sparkling eyes.

    A single blue butterfly

gliding on a rainforest breeze.

    A ray beam of sunshine

on a spring time morning.

    A sneaky little hug in bed

during a winter's storm.

    A smirk of lips and roll of eyes

as mum did something silly.

    A burst of laughter with rolling tears

over a silly joke that's given.

    Loud arguments with her siblings

but protecting them from others.

A rainbow brightly glowing

during a springtime shower.

A light gentle breeze in summer

whilst laying on the trampoline.

A smile given late at night

hiding under the warm blankets.

A sapling young and nimble

bent over backwards touching ground.

An energy, a life, a soul, a friend

annoying, loving, joyful vitality.

She was daylight, warmth and caring.

She was bright sunshine.

She was Kayleigh.

She was.

Notes

Challenge

This poem was written with my son Lucas' input. This was his favourite memory of Kayleigh, playing Mario Kart in his room against his brothers and sisters and absolutely beating Kayleigh, who would get annoyed that her baby brother was so good – she was 8 years older than Lucas.

Face Plant

This poem was written about one of Terry's memories of Kayleigh. Her bike was a little worn out, with brakes that took a long time to slow her down. Terry got a new bike that year for Christmas, that looked a bit like a motorbike, and Terry warned her multiple times to be careful with the brakes. She didn't listen to him, and went tearing down the driveway before slamming on the brakes and stacking the bike because it stopped so fast. Terry thought it hilarious – a real told you so moment.

Rats!

Kiara was only 4 when Kayleigh passed, her memories are not as well formed as her older siblings, but Rats is certainly one she remembers clearly. Kiara had received a copy of the latest Tinkerbell movie on Christmas, which had a scary scene with rats in it. Kayleigh used this to get Kiara to behave – rats under the trampoline to get Kiara to get onto the trampoline, rats on the bedroom floor to ensure that Kiara would stay in bed.

Skywards

Kayleigh, Natassja and their friend Alexandra all used to climb trees. There was a particular tree on their walk home every afternoon that they loved to climb up – to see how high they could go. This poem is based on Natassjas memory of those days.

Dragons

In her last year, Kayleigh really got into drawing dragons, tracing and retracing them, taking out and removing parts she didn't like. She gave her teacher Mr Haidon two drawings of dragons – an ice dragon and a fire dragon – which Natassja has reproduced for this poem.

Somebody

Somebody was written in the months after Kayleighs' death, and was included in a blog I wrote during that time. I have included in as written as part of this book of poems about her passing.

Afterward

Death is inevitable.
Grief is eternal.

Thank you for taking the opportunity for reading my words. This book was difficult to write, and I understand that many of my readers will find it difficult to read. Please be kind to yourselves, take a break, sit on a hilltop, wander through a field. Life is here for the living, and while grief is a part of our lives, it should never be ones' life either.

Grieving is a process, and everyone does it differently. It also lasts a lifetime. I can be fine one week, and the next day my loss feels like it just happened just yesterday. Remember those who you have lost, live for today, and be kind to yourself, and others.

Much love,

JL Herald

I love you lots

Love Kayleigh.

In memory

Kayleigh Lucille Stamp

14th December 1996

—

4th June 2010

About the Author

JL Herald grew up in Canberra, Australia and has a Bachelor of Social Sciences from the University of Canberra. The mother of six children, she currently still has three at home along with her 2 cats, Sox and Eevee, and her beagle Sherlock.

Her first book *toxic/empathy* was published in 2024, and she re-published her great (x4)-grandfathers Alexander Herald's poetry book *Amusements of Solitude* in 2024.

www.ingramcontent.com/pod-product-compliance
Lightning Source LLC
Chambersburg PA
CBHW051453290426
44109CB00016B/1741